50¢

D0121793

plates

MARY ENGELBREIT'S
HOME
COMPANION

plates

Text by Vitta Poplar

Photography by Barbara Elliott Martin

Andrews McMeel
Publishing
Kansas City

Plates copyright © 1999 by Mary Engelbreit Ink
Photographs © 1999 Universal Engelbreit Cox

All rights reserved. No part of this book may be used or reproduced in any manner whatsoever without written permission except in the case of reprints in the context of reviews. For information, write Andrews McMeel Publishing, an Andrews McMeel Universal company, 4520 Main Street, Kansas City, Missouri 64111.

www.andrewsmcmeel.com
www.maryengelbreit.com

, Mary Engelbreit, and Mary Engelbreit's Home Companion are registered trademarks of Mary Engelbreit Enterprises, Inc.

Library of Congress Cataloging-in-Publication Data
Engelbreit, Mary.
    [Home companion]
    Mary Engelbreit's home companion : plates / text by Vitta Poplar ;
photography by Barbara Elliott Martin.
        p.   cm.
    ISBN 0-7407-0201-7
    1. Plates (Tableware)--Collectors and collecting--United States.
    I. Poplar, Vitta.   II. Martin, Barbara Elliott.   III. Title
    NK8596.E54   1999
    642' .7--dc21   99-35411
                                                                        CIP

10 9 8 7 6 5 4 3 2 1

MARY ENGELBREIT'S HOME COMPANION
Editor in Chief: Mary Engelbreit
Executive Editor: Barbara Elliott Martin
Art Director: Marcella Spanogle

Produced by SMALLWOOD & STEWART, INC., New York City

Printed in Great Britain by Butler & Tanner Ltd., Frome and London

ATTENTION: SCHOOLS AND BUSINESSES
Andrews McMeel books are available at quantity discounts with bulk purchase for educational, business, or sales promotional use. For information, please write to: Special Sales Department, Andrews McMeel Publishing, 4520 Main Street, Kansas City, Missouri 64111.

contents

introduction

THERE'S HARDLY A PLATE that I can walk by without picking it up, turning it over, and examining every detail. It can take me hours to get through a flea market! I care less about the monetary value of a piece than that it have a special something—a wonderful color, a whimsical pattern, a detailed rendition of a scene.

And I don't just use plates to serve meals. I hang them on my walls, stack them on a side table, display them in a hutch, use them to brighten up a dark corner. They are just as versatile as artwork—perhaps even more so, since you don't need to worry about frames. Of course, mealtime with plates is great fun, too, when you can pull out a set just right for the occasion—pretty ones for a wedding shower, elegant ones for a holiday dinner, colorful ones for a barbecue.

Whether you decide to create a collection of a particular kind of plate—say, Fiestaware—or to display an eclectic one of myriad styles and patterns, I hope you will enjoy them as much as I do.

Mary Engelbreit

7

chapter one

THE MORE THE M

We're all accidental plate collectors at one time or another. Our first experience of collecting might come when we raid our parents' cabinets to stock our dorm room or first apartment, or haul off a box of dishes at a yard sale to host a dinner party. Plates are such everyday objects that it's easy to take them for granted. But once you start paying attention, admiring those little floral details and pretty scallops on the rim, you inevitably start acquiring plates not just for utilitarian purposes, but for their beauty. Something captures your eye—whether it's a particular maker, pattern, or theme, like blue-and-white or roses—and you find yourself acquiring more and more.

Like the old lady who lived in a shoe, collectors of children's plates often have so many, they don't know what to do. Fortunately, your home is probably larger than your shoe size, so you can devote an entire cupboard to these small dishes. Their transfer-printed nursery rhyme scenes and embossed ABCs are playful decorations for any room.

what's your fancy?

THERE'S A PLATE theme to satisfy every collector—holiday plates, souvenir plates, botanically themed plates. One of the most popular themes is baby plates, which were made specifically for youngsters to use at the table (unlike plates made for playing with dolls). Some collectors call them ABC plates, a reference to the alphabet letters, often embossed, that run around the rims of the bowls. Most date from the late 18th through the 19th century and were imported from England. They could be made of porcelain, pottery, pewter, or tin and invariably had a nursery rhyme or picture in the center, whether of the pie man selling his wares at the fair or children playing on a seesaw. Though some were painted by hand, most had transfer-printed designs, in multiple colors.

Some baby plates also paired maxims with appropriate scenes, such as "He That Hath a Trade Hath an Estate," and the surprisingly modern, "There Are No Gains Without Pain" (with a picture of men at work in a field).

Children's ware, another category, was made by English and German firms from as early as the 17th century. These miniature china sets were intended both as playthings for children and as tools for teaching dining etiquette.

Christmas plates are one of the unsung joys of the holiday season. The first were made in 1895 by Bing and Grondahl, the Danish porcelain maker; Royal Copenhagen began making holiday plates in 1908. The collectible appeal of these plates stems from the fact that a limited number are made in a particular style, then the molds are broken. Often the plates recreate a scene—for instance, a Christmas tree glimpsed through a frosty window, the Little Match Girl from the Hans Christian Andersen tale, or a skating couple. There is usually a date, as well, for authenticity.

Souvenir plates are well-suited for display—they take to walls and cabinets like station wagons to rest stops.

From the late 1800s through the 1930s, Germany and Austria produced most of the American souvenir plates. If that's not surprising enough, these early wares were true porcelain. Decorated with scenes of small town America, some even handpainted in multiple colors, they were often made for merchants to promote their businesses, or to commemorate carnivals, fairs, and expositions.

After World War II, as families took to the road in record numbers, famous landmarks such as Niagara Falls and vacation states like California and Florida became popular subjects on plates made mostly by the Japanese.

all the world
on a plate

matthew 5:13

you are the salt of the earth.

Some collectors display
their plates bottoms up
to show off the marks.
Circles, stars, arrows,
crowns, shields, suns,
triangles, hearts, and
towers are among the
intricate symbols—and
each one silently tells
its own story.

on your
marks

THERE'S A CERTAIN POETRY and romance to plate marks. The mix of cryptic symbols, numbers, and initials is undeniably intriguing. And it is possible to crack the code. If a plate bears only the name of the country where it was made, it most likely dates from after 1890. This was the year the United States instituted a law that all imported wares be labeled with the country name. When the country of origin is prefaced by the words "Made in . . . ," the piece was made after 1914. Plates made in Japan provide you with even more clues to age: If the piece is inscribed with the word Nippon (equivalent of "Japan" in Japanese), then it was made between the years 1891 and 1921. In 1921, the U.S. government ruled that the word Japan replace Nippon.

Often, no country name appears. In this case, check out the mark itself. The earliest marks were pretty basic, so a good rule of thumb is the more intricate the mark, the newer the piece. Also, if the plate has no "rim" on the bottom, it is probably pre–19th century. If you see the word "trademark," the piece is English and dates from 1855 or after. If you see the letters "LTD," it is English and dates from 1880 or later.

out on a
rim

WHO CAN RESIST piercework on a plate's rim? We can all thank Leeds Pottery of Yorkshire, England, which operated from roughly 1760 to the 1870s, for initiating this welcome trend. Its luscious cream-colored earthenware was meticulously cut by hand punches, hole by hole. The results were so special, they were prized on par with porcelain. Diamonds, hearts, lozenges, and petals appeared in combinations so lacy and fine it looked like each plate border was painstakingly stitched together.

Though Leeds creamware can be pricey, take heart: There's always milk glass, the 19th century's affordable porcelain substitute, pressed in the same molds as clear glass. Designs include shell dishes flanked by gothic arched handles and crimped ruffles, heart-shaped candy dishes surrounded by pierced hearts and arrows, and torte servers with lattice-work borders. Milk glass poured out of major glasshouses into the 1980s, so there is plenty to choose from.

When pierced border plates decorate a wall or sit upright on a plate stand, something magic happens: Their patterns extend to the wall space beyond, decorating it with a dance of shadow and light.

Small, gem-like plates, like this leaf-shaped candy dish (above), are best appreciated at eye level.

A trio of plates (right), with the largest at center, satisfies the eye's love of balance.

Thirties milk glass with cutwork rims contours the curved back of an overstuffed armchair (left). The plates were deliberately designed to be displayed with ribbons woven around the edges, but this collector "gift wraps" them with bows instead.

Just as a frame calls attention to a work of art, a plate with an intriguing rim (above) can turn simple objects such as candy, marbles, or seashells into tiny treasures worthy of a closer look. White plates always make a perfect foil for colorful contents.

Displayed with precious
Oriental pottery on
a neoclassical table, a
prized porcelain plate
invites passersby to slow
down and have a look.
Note the clever use of
a mirror behind the
plate, so that its front
and back are visible at
the same time.

by any other name

ANY OBJECT MADE FROM fired clay falls under the definition of ceramics. Within that category, there is a great deal of terminology (and confusion), and it all has to do with the type of clay that is used and the temperature at which the clay is fired. Basically, there are two broad divisions: porcelain and earthenware, which is also called pottery (British collectors sometimes use the term pottery to include porcelain, but for our purposes, it is interchangeable with earthenware).

Porcelain is considered the most high-end ceramic of all and is the true "china," even though china has become an all-purpose term. A quick way to identify porcelain is simply to hold the piece up to a bright light: If it is translucent and you can see your fingers on the other side, then you are likely holding a piece of porcelain (unless it's glass, of course!).

Today's porcelain collectors continue the "chinamania" tradition started by 17th-century royalty—most notably Queen Mary of England—who filled their palaces with the rare ceramic from the Orient. For centuries, making porcelain had been a Chinese secret. When European producers finally unlocked the formula in the 18th century (add kaolin,

Beaded-edge porcelain with handpainted sprays of spring flowers (above) is precious indeed— the china was inherited from the owner's mother-in-law. But that doesn't mean it's kept under lock and key. Instead, the service is used for Sunday dinners and family occasions.

Plate racks (right) are a collector's best friend, enabling you to keep everyday earthenware dishes and mugs at the ready while at the same time serving as decorations.

a fine white clay, to china stone and decomposed granite and fire at an extremely high temperature), many makers sprang up all over England and the Continent. The first Western attempts at porcelain produced soft-paste porcelain— translucent, but because of its clay composition and lower firing temperature not as durable as hard-paste porcelain.

Another famous type of porcelain is bone china. Somewhere between hard- and soft-paste porcelain in composition, it includes calcined animal bones in the mix. Bone china was purportedly invented by Josiah Spode in the late 18th century and, thanks to its reasonable price, was immediately popular.

Unlike porcelain, earthenware is opaque, and more easily broken. The earliest form of tableware, from the 16th century onward earthenware came in many variations, including slipware (coarse clay decorated with more clay watered down to the consistency of cream), delftware (tin-glazed earthenware), and stoneware (intensely hard earthenware fired at a higher temperature than others).

If you're an antiquer, you've doubtless seen the word "ironstone" in your travels. The Englishman Charles James Mason patented this heavy, thick earthenware in 1813 and gave it its name. (Other producers would call it white granite, stone china, semi-china, and other misleading names.) The earliest plates were simple circles, but the designs became fancier as the century progressed. Later-made plates are more likely to have raised border designs; most were embellished with transfer prints.

ceramics is the catchall name

tender loving
care

CARING FOR YOUR OLDER plates requires a few simple precautions. Any dish that has gold or lustre decorations or hairline cracks, or is "crazed" (with a network of tiny, visible cracks in the glaze) or repaired in some way must be washed by hand. First line the sink with towels so that if a plate slips, you can avert disaster. Use an ordinary sponge to clean plates, unless you have an especially precious older plate with chips. In that case, remove loose dirt that has fallen into the cracks with a soft artist's brush. Then dip cotton balls in a solution of mild detergent and use them to gently hand-wash the plate in lukewarm water. Dry with a soft towel. If an antique dish is stained or if it starts to come apart at the glue join it's time to call in a professional restorer. Never try to bleach out stains from an old plate.

Of course, if your plates are of more recent vintage, then a dishwasher will often do. Just don't subject the plates to extremes of temperature—for instance, plunging a hot dish into cold water. When storing or transporting plates, stack like sizes and shapes together. Use tissue paper to separate the layers, or felt to prevent scratching.

Damaged by a California earthquake, this Japanese hand-painted plate was restored by its owner and now sits squarely on a stand—with a small chunk missing. For simple repairs, use a craft store superglue that contains cyanoacrylate ester. If you need to fill gaps, use epoxy resin. When a plate is broken beyond repair, explore other alternatives: Mortar the pieces onto a birdbath in a mosaic, or among the tiles in a kitchen backsplash.

chapter two

ON DISPLAY

If you're wedded to the idea of displaying your china only facing out into the room on walls and in hutches, think again. Marcy Spanogle, art director of MARY ENGELBREIT'S HOME COMPANION magazine, reminds us that plates were made for tables—and for chairs. "I redecorate my kitchen just by moving around stacks of bowls and dishes," she says. "One week I'll have an ivory theme, the next week, blue and green."

Call them what you like: plate-scapes, dish towers—they're a charming way to play rims off one another. One beauty of decorating with plates: You can show them off in steamy kitchens and baths, and sun-splashed spaces where fragile, framed artwork fears to tread.

put the best
face forward

Side-stacking plate racks (above) allow you to contrast interesting rims, but when plates show full scenes, as with historic Staffordshire or Blue Willow, opt to display them in a hutch (opposite), so they can be admired face on.

TAKE A STROLL THROUGH your rooms with a fresh eye. There's hardly a corner that won't take to a plate or two. Imagine a guest's surprise in finding an exquisite polka-dot dish of candies on the night table. Or the pleasure you'll take in admiring your favorite souvenir plate from the comfort of your own bathtub.

There's no need to limit plate racks or hutches to the kitchen and dining room when you can put one on your screened porch to hold your favorite alfresco dinnerware. Even children's rooms are candidates for plate decorating: Hung free-form on the wall, doll-size dishes look like bubbles blown from a pipe. (For tiny plates like these, you can adapt a traditional spring-type wall hanger: Just shorten the spring with a snip of a wire cutter to adjust it to the plate's size.) Adult bedrooms can be set ashimmer with lus-treware, which looks as dreamy by dawn glow as it does by candlelight. Or fashion a headboard of plates arranged in an arc over the bed. And in the living room, instead of an oil painting over your sofa, substitute plates grouped in an oval, circle, or square. Mix and match plates with similar hues but varied shapes from any era, just as you would at the table.

The next time you want to frame a photo, consider the saucer. Its central cranny is perfect for displaying a small portrait, trimmed to size and adhered with a glue stick. In this clever arrangement (above), Chinese newspaper, cut in deep scallops with pinking shears, is hung from the shelf above, like a curtain rising on a stage.

In Mary's former dining room (right), a painted swag frames a quartet of botanical dessert plates, arranged in a gentle arc.

Handpainted by Jill Rosenwald, porcelain salad plates make charming decorations for a wall (left). One advantage of ordering from an artist is that you can often choose your own colors and designs to perfectly complement other furnishings.

When an awkward space like the narrow area above a window (above) cries out for something—anything—to enliven it, consider adding a plate or two.

Pewter chargers spaced along a rail perfectly complement the earthy tones and emphasis on natural materials of the Arts and Crafts aesthetic.

match
a mood

WHATEVER YOUR STYLE, a plate awaits. Perhaps
you're an incurable romantic and adore English chintz
and all things botanical. Then by all means serve up
platters of porcelain roses on the walls and let dishes in
a chintzy pattern, like Johnson Bros. "Rose Chintz," act
as catchalls for barrettes, buttons, and keys.

If the fresh, breezy look of blue and white touches
every detail of your home—tiles, curtains, pillows—it
is only natural to carry the theme through to your china.
Chinoiserie, delft, faience, supermarket giveaways—they
all go together. Of course, if you collect the 1950s, you're
really in luck: Perch a "California Mobile" platter from
Metlox on your boomerang coffee table. Dine on Fiestaware and Harlequin. In the kitchen, hang a sectional plate
depicting a barbecuing couple in full kitsch glory. And if
it's your grandmother's old chenille bedspreads and hand-
embroidered linens you adore, then the sparkling soft tones
of Depression glass will suit your retro rooms.

Reaching further back into the past, red-and-white
transferware plates hung directly on the sides of beams are a
good match to warm up traditional colonial interiors.

East meets West in a California bungalow (above). Blue-and-white Chinese porcelain flows from table to wall, while the couch blends English chintz with French toile. How does it all come together so effortlessly?

Harmonious patterns and complementary colors are the key.

Antique blue-and-white Spode resides in an old English bookcase (opposite) while a dumb-waiter offers a selection of gilt-rimmed plates.

This Asian-influenced porcelain (left) follows in a long tradition of Oriental export ware, prized for its vivid hues like mandarin, enamel blue, and chrysanthemum. Displayed against a subdued ivory wall, the colors pop like firecrackers on Chinese New Year. In keeping with the Eastern aesthetic, established by a backdrop of Japanese obis draped on a kimono stand, the table is set with brilliantly colored plates that seem to have danced off the fabric. The medallion at center and the four floral panels ornamenting the edges of the plates (detail above) are classic Canton-ware motifs.

creating
a tableau

Intricate patterns of old transferware "frame" a display of amber and leopard-print candles (above), conjuring a heady mood of exotic adventure.

You can practically hear the waves when you gaze on sea-themed English transferware paired with nautical artifacts (opposite).

THINK ABOUT YOUR favorite china: There's probably a story connected to it. Maybe you bought it on a trip to Europe, in a potter's workshop in New Mexico, or on a charmed flea market outing where everything seemed to call out to you. Perhaps you inherited a favorite plate, or one was given to you by a friend because it reflects your passion for purple.

Rather than displaying your treasures in isolation, weave a story around them. That rose-sprinkled Limoges porcelain you got on your honeymoon abroad would look lovely hung on the wall alongside framed maps of the French countryside, tracing your route. Show off your majolica basketweave platter covered with strawberries in a garden tableau, perhaps alongside a vintage galvanized watering can and old hand cultivators. And Great-Grandmother's 1920s china—the complete eight-piece setting—looks happy on a sideboard with her portrait, silver perfume flasks, and a shadowbox pastiche of mementos: her train ticket to Niagara Falls, the jewelry she wore, a letter she wrote.

Such tableaux lift plates out of the realm of utility and into a story—one that is yours alone to tell.

every plate tells a story

Built-in shelves provide the stage setting for earthy-colored sponge-ware, cattail-themed chargers, and slim tortoiseshell-finished boxes (left).

In a woodsy home near Atlanta, Edwardian plates with portraits of deer, elk, and moose make the perfect counterpoint to outdoor paraphernalia (above), including a fishing creel and oars. Note how the smaller, circular plates orbit the oval platter: the eye naturally loves a larger focal point.

In Rose Hicks's family room, prized milk glass is reflected in a strategically placed mirror, itself flanked by leaf-shaped candy dishes, whose raised rims add texture and shadow play to the walls. On the coffee table, a platter safeguards a vase and figurine.

a plate maven's
haven

WHEN CHINA COLLECTING was the rage in the early 18th century, collectors would devote a room to porcelain alone, even embedding ceramics right in the wall. For modern-day plate lover Rose Hicks of Fredericksburg, Texas, one room is not enough: She designed her entire home around her favorite dishes.

A paint and furnishings palette of cream, straw, cane, and taupe complements dishware displayed throughout her home. Everywhere you turn, platters and saucers act as catchalls for family photos, potpourri, buttons, vases, and other odds and ends. Over the living room couch, circles, scallops, and ovals rub rims in a free-form puzzle that includes a botanical painting. In one tabletop tableau, cream-colored china clusters with crystal.

In her family room, Rose even painted her mahogany Duncan Phyfe occasional table white to match her plates, then proceeded on to the dining room to transform her pine chairs with a crackle glaze, mimicking the crazed pattern on the china in her breakfront. But it is in her bedroom that her love of dishes is best served: A plate decorated with her year of birth hangs opposite the bed,

Plates, plates, every-
where: Brown transfer-
ware plates inspired the
use of rich-toned wood
in the bath (right); the
sink is a converted
bachelor's chest. Rose's
only baby picture is
propped up by butter-
beans on a bedside
platter (below). And a
tiny half moon relish
dish hovers intriguingly
over the living room's
plate and painting
pastiche (far right).

"All pale china gets along"

while the soft blue walls were inspired by a platter decorated with bluebirds.

"Plates in pale shades are perfect when you want to
play up texture and form over color," says Hicks. "They
decorate a room in a way that paintings never could—
they're wonderful to look at, yet they don't make your
eyes 'work' to appreciate them. The effect is so soothing."

Rose painted her pine dining room breakfront white (opposite), then let her daughter Janet decoupage the interior with pages from an old book. In a perfect example of creating a tableau, Rose sprinkled in stacks of childhood books among the plates, indicating her longtime dedication to both. Another wonderful touch in the dining room: A small saucer suspended from wire (above and detail left) adds a further devotional message to a framed Bible page.

Collected both stateside and abroad on the cheap, Jane Keltner's plates depict international flora and fauna and even an Italian monastery (shown on the plate at center).

it's in the
mix

"ANYTHING TO DECLARE?" asks the customs agent. "Well, just a whole set of French porcelain," answers Jane Keltner, eager to get back to her Memphis, Tennessee, home with her latest booty.

The inspector momentarily raises an eyebrow at Jane's purchase price—just a few francs—but then waves her on. Had he insisted on proof, she would have pointed out the minimal chipping under the rims, which makes them far less valuable than the casual observer might think.

"I would *never* spend a lot of money on plates," says this color-loving furniture designer and painter. "Especially when they're destined for my walls—after all, accidents do happen."

In fact, Jane is not so much after plate perfection, but a color theme. In the case of the plates opposite, the raison d'etre of her composition was lemon-lime. A yellow Palladian window-turned-shelf contrasts with the wall's fruity kiwi hue, and the mostly English plates positioned spoke-side add extra flavor twists to the mix.

"I am a furniture designer, after all, so I start with the big pieces and let the plates fall where they may."

"Let plates fall where they may"

Though she seeks out bargains whenever possible, Jane will also indulge in a new artist-made plate like these handpainted peapods (above). "Since I love all things green, I couldn't resist them," she says. "Green is one of those colors that has an old-timey feel, so it's easy to blend old and new." For instance, English ivy plates (right) from the 1920s meld with more contemporary furnishings. "Never force your plates into a 'spot' in your house," says Jane. "If you wait long enough, they'll find their place."

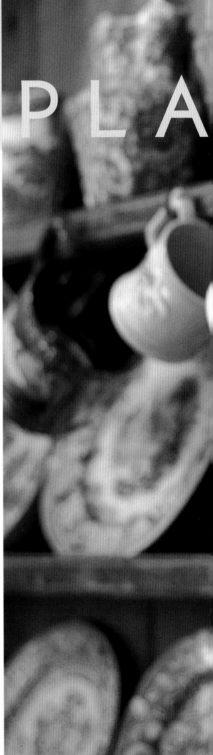

chapter three

A PLETHORA OF PLA

Building a plate collection is one of life's joys. Finding a mate for a pink transferware dish, getting a new Audubon plate every Christmas—once you get started, you're hooked. As with any collectible, buy the best condition you can afford. For obvious flaws such as glaze flaking away or chipping, let the price reflect the degree of the damage. Some collectors would never purchase a piece of crazed china—in which a network of tiny cracks is visible—but others find this feature charming, a mark of age, and an intriguing pattern in itself. Once you know the fine points of what you're collecting, then you can build upon it with confidence.

collecting
enamelware

YOU PROBABLY GREW UP with a piece or two of old enamelware kicking around the kitchen. Maybe it was your mother's roasting pan, a robin's egg blue design with tiny white speckles. Or the old green-and-white-swirled coffeepot that the family took camping.

Also known as graniteware or agateware, enamelware has been a kitchen standard from the late 19th century to the present. It is basically enameled tinware, and shouldn't be confused with spongeware, or spatterware, which is earthenware. The first domestic enamelware designs tended to be green or turquoise, covered with white speckling or mottling. Grays, greens, purples, and deeper blues were later popular colors. French-made wares are usually more graphic, with checkerboard patterns and handpainted florals and fruits.

There are plenty of enamelware collecting possibilities: Imagine a wall display that includes a cobalt saucer, a purple pie plate with white speckles, and a white muffin tin with snappy black trim. Since enamelware isn't fragile, the supply is plentiful. And you can easily (and inexpensively) round out an old collection with the many new designs being created today.

Enamelware was designed for utility first, looks second, so don't hesitate to put it to work as a festive centerpiece, complete with excelsior and American flags (left).

In Mary's former kitchen, a grouping of tin-enameled plates and bowls (above) catches the eye with a fruits-and-flowers theme.

collecting
transferware

TO PLATE COLLECTORS, the word transferware is synonymous with the name of the place it comes from, Staffordshire, England. Staffordshire is a district, not a single factory; in fact, hundreds of factories have operated in Staffordshire since the mid 18th century, when it became the center of the pottery industry.

Pictures of historic events and romantic scenery characterize transferware. Designs are engraved onto a copper plate, then transferred to paper, which is wrapped around the china (sometimes porcelain but most often earthenware); when the piece is fired, the paper burns off. It was invented as a cheaper alternative to Chinese handpainted porcelain and therefore often featured Asian motifs.

Early in the 19th century, the transfer designs tended to be a combination of European and Oriental motifs: for instance, a Continental-style floral border with a pagoda scene at center. Transfer prints could be repeated on the interior of the plate, and patched in—sometimes a bit unevenly—to fit the space.

As the century progressed, the print designs became more refined, taking on more subtle shadings and having a more three-dimensional effect. Scenic views not just of the

In a Texas breakfast room, Blue Willow ties everything together (opposite). You'll even find it on the old Toby jugs and cow creamers in the tiny wall-hung cabinet and on the china base of the sideboard lamp. Generations have feasted on the familiar bridge, tree, and bird pattern (above).

This transferware grouping (above) appears to be freeform, but look again: Twin plates play off each other in the middle, and soup bowls anchor the bottom. Proving that pattern invites more pattern, a gingham curtain and floral tablecloth balance the breakfast nook look.

In a cherry red hutch, scenic blue transferware comes to life (opposite).

Orient but of romantic European destinations, peppered with castles and towers, became popular. England also churned out many American scenes on its china, especially from about 1820 to 1840.

Within the category of transferware, there is also the curious—and huge—division of willowware, or Blue Willow china, produced by hundreds of makers, to this day, in both earthenware and porcelain. Blue Willow looks about as Oriental as you can get, and collectors say the story it tells, that of a cruel father and star-crossed lovers, is based on an authentic Chinese myth. However, it's quite possible that this is entirely an English invention.

Thomas Minton is credited with creating the first piece in the 1780s, "Willow-Nankin," and Josiah Spode elaborated upon it a decade later, finally arriving at what we would recognize as Blue Willow in 1810: a willow tree pictured with a tea house and a bridge over a lake. On the bridge are three figures, island bound, while a man sits in a boat on the lake. Two birds fly across the top, toward each other. Geometric designs frame the entire rim.

After Spode set the scene, more than two hundred other makers, from such diverse countries as Belgium, Ireland, Mexico, and Poland, jumped in with their own interpretations. No wonder there seems to be no end to Blue Willow—and the pleasure it gives. Don't be misled by Blue Willow's name: Though it is usually blue, you'll also come across mulberry, black, yellow, brown, green, and polychrome.

collecting
depressior

Lacy Depression glass looks lovely with pastels, like these egg-cups blooming with daffodils (above).

A large window (opposite) is the ideal place for displaying Depression glass—or any glass!—since light sets it aglow. These amber luncheon and dinner plates seem made for special effects at sunset.

NO ONE CALLED IT Depression glass when it was being made. And no one paid it any mind, either: It was simply inexpensive machine-made glassware produced in the 1920s and 1930s by dozens of American factories, and often given away on "Dish Night" at the local movie house when talkies were young.

Of course, contemporary collectors are positively jubilant when they come across Depression glass. Prized today for its lacy, bubbly, or banded patterns and barley candy colors, this retro kitchen staple is a joy to collect and display. The pattern names are cute to boot: "American Sweetheart," "Cherryberry," "Cube," "Floragold," "Waffle," and "Pretzel" are just a taste.

Where to begin your hunt? Search your own cupboards first: Everyone seems to have a piece or two hidden away. Then keep your eyes wide open in your travels—you'll recognize Depression ware instantly by its playful sparkle and distinctive colors: pink, amber, cobalt blue, red, yellow, white, crystal, amethyst, ultramarine, and forest or pale green. Some of the glass was opalescent, notably "Beaded Block" by Imperial Glass Corporation of Bellaire, Ohio, and "Moonstone" by Anchor Hocking of Lancaster, Ohio.

glass

collecting
majolica

MAJOLICA DATES TO MEDIEVAL Italy, when it was an everyday pottery glazed with an opaque tin enamel in wonderful purples and coppery greens. It is sometimes still spelled "maiolica," in deference to its Italian origins.

But it was in the 19th century that majolica as we know it appeared in all its quirky glory: Herbert Minton of England started the craze, calling his brightly colored pottery with heavy relief "majolica" to give it the cachet of the old Italian kind. Then makers from all over England, Europe, and America started to turn out similar whimsical wares, usually painted by unskilled labor.

English producers often added their marks, particularly Minton and Wedgwood, and many majolica pieces are identified by country of origin. However, much of U.S. majolica is completely unmarked, with the exception of the products of two firms. The words "Etruscan Majolica" or the abbreviation "GSH" indicates it was made by Griffen, Smith and Hill of Phoenixville, Pennsylvania. If you see the words "Avalon" or "Clifton," it's produced by Chesapeake Pottery of Baltimore, Maryland. Even if it's unmarked, don't expect majolica to go cheaply. The majolica craze is still alive and well.

Some majolica practically tells you how to use it: A Wedgwood trout platter, sectional oyster plate made from "shells," and sardine boxes topped by sea creatures give strong hints (opposite).

Majolica leaf plates abound (above). The cabbage creamer at front is first cousin to artichoke-shaped bowls and lilypad-clad pitchers.

collecting
fire-king

"INEXPENSIVE, HEAT-RESISTANT, rugged, stain-resistant, sanitary, colorful," boasted Anchor Hocking of its popular Fire-King glasswares, made from the 1940s through the 1970s.

Collectors have a penchant for jadeite, Fire-King's most recognizable hue, an ethereal green. It was the color of the 1950s Restaurant Ware line that included wonderful cereal bowls with wide flanged rims, compartment plates, plates with cup indents, and large oval platters. Hocking also produced other Fire-King lines in forest green, gray laurel, pink, turquoise blue, and clear glass. From the lacy "Alice" pattern of the 1940s to the square "Charm" series of the early 1950s and the white "Primrose" decal pattern of the 1960s, the styles and shapes reflect their eras.

But the pattern that is synonymous with Fire-King is "Jane Ray," made from 1945 to 1963 and identified by the ribbed rim on its plates and saucers, as well as on the lids and sides of sugar bowls and the sides of cups. Aside from jadeite, it came in ivory, peach lustre, and white. Like most of the Fire-King lines, it is designed to go from oven to table, but cautious collectors keep their Fire-King respectfully far from the flame.

When you collect a single era, it's easy to mix pieces from different makers. A case in point: 1940s Fire-King plates seem made for a Fiesta pitcher (above).

A jadeite "Jane Ray" sugarbowl scoops attention on the middle shelf (opposite); the cereal bowls stacked on the bottom shelf are also Fire-King.

collecting
lustreware

EVERYONE CAN PICK LUSTREWARE out of a
china lineup: Its shimmer seems to beckon you to touch it,
hold it in your hand. Made for centuries in different cultures,
this prized ceramic gets its bewitching glow from a thin
metallic glaze.

Throughout the 19th century, English potteries applied
lustre glazes to earthenware and bone china to make them
resemble silver, gold, and copper. They also experimented
with purely decorative effects, especially on tea sets.
Wedgwood pioneered "moonlight lustre," achieved by mix-
ing various tints of purple, and several factories produced a
"splash" lustre, which involved spraying oil on wet lustre,
resulting in an intriguing bubble effect in the kiln. The
embossed fruits running round the rim of the famous
Chelsea-grape pattern dishes were often decorated with
purple, lavender, or blue lustre.

From the 1920s through the 1940s, the Japanese revived
lustreware for the masses, creating affordable and whimsical
Deco-style pieces. You'll recognize these wares not only by
their fluid lines and designs—stylized posies, storybook
houses, elegant ladies—but also by their marks: Nippon,
Made in Japan, or a large M surrounded by a wreath.

Though all basically
the same citrus shade—
with generous purple
accents—each of these
lustreware pieces (oppo-
site) sports its own
motif, from Japanese
fishermen to Oriental
flowers.

An apple green glaze
and stylized illustration
identify this plate (above)
as Art Deco lustreware.

Mary's Deco lustreware collection inspired the sherbet-hued decor of her former living room, where 1940s-style floral pillows accent the seating. The iridescent colors would also harmonize with an interior filled with shimmery raw silk textiles. To preserve its glaze, keep lustreware out of direct sunlight—just as Mary tucked hers into a built-in bookcase.

collecting
fiestaware

CONCEIVED AS A CASUAL LINE that would harmonize with most any decor, Fiesta was introduced by the Homer Laughlin China Company in 1936. Art Deco in style, the streamlined pottery was in tune with the times and an immediate success. The original eleven colors were chartreuse, old ivory, cobalt, dark green, light green, medium green, gray, red, rose, turquoise, and yellow.

Plate collectors can have a field day with Fiesta, choosing from such specialized wares as chop plates, celery trays, and compartment plates. Of course, the company offered the plates as part of complete dinnerware sets, including such novelty items as covered onion soup bowls, tripod candle holders, demitasse pots, and marmalade jars.

Though Homer Laughlin retired the Fiesta line in 1972, the company reintroduced it in 1986 with a few different colors: pale yellow, lilac, white, persimmon, and sea mist green among them. Cobalt and turquoise are still part of the line, but darker than the original shades. Also, the newer wares are made from vitrified china, which is denser than the semivitrified china of the originals. The new wave of Fiesta ensures a healthy supply of collectibles well into the 21st century.

Frederick Rhead, the Fiesta designer, likened the semi-reflective glazed surface of his creation to that of a billiard ball. It was intended to provide instant cheer to tabletops (above).

A gift to a Fiesta lover by her artistic mother, this tiny dinnerware set (opposite) is faithful to the colors and styles of the real thing.

getting the goods

antiques stores

The Brass Armadillo
12419 North 28th Drive
Phoenix, AZ 85029
(888) 942-0030

Santa Monica Antique Market
1607 Lincoln Boulevard
Santa Monica, CA 90404
(310) 314-4899

Central Park Antique Mall
701 19th Street
Bakersfield, CA 93301
(661) 633-1143

Heirlooms Antique Mall
327 East Main Street
Ventura, CA 93001
(805) 648-4833

Newport Avenue Antique Center
4864 Newport Avenue
San Diego, CA 92107
(619) 222-8686

Missouri Valley Antiques
1931 Highway 30
Missouri Valley, IA 51555
(712) 642-2125

The Brass Armadillo
701 N.E. 50th Avenue
Des Moines, IA 50313
(515) 262-0092

Great Midwestern Antique Emporium
5233 Dixie Highway
Waterford, MI 48329
(248) 623-7460

Glass Turtle
2112 Cherokee
St. Louis, MO 61118
(314) 771-6779

Stone Ledge Antiques
P.O. Box 110
Dutzow, MO 63342
(314) 458-3516

Tommy T's
3010 Sutton Boulevard
St. Louis, MO 63143
(314) 645-7471

Warson Woods Antique Gallery
10091 Manchester Road
St. Louis, MO 63122
(314) 909-0123

The Brass Armadillo
10666 Sapp Brothers Drive
Omaha, NE 68138
(800) 896-9140

Chelsea Antiques Building
110 West 25th Street
New York, NY 10001
(212) 929-0909

MacKenzie-Childs, Ltd.
824 Madison Avenue
New York, NY 10021
(212) 570-6050

Becky Portera Antiques
2710 McKinney Avenue
Dallas, TX 75204
(214) 871-9803

Homestead
223 East Main St.
Fredericksburg, TX 78624
(800) 670-0729

antiques and flea markets

Long Beach Outdoor Antique and Collectible Market
Long Beach Veterans Stadium
Long Beach, CA
(323) 655-5703

Rose Bowl Flea Market
1001 Rose Bowl Drive
Pasadena, CA
(323) 560-7469

San Bernadino Outdoor Market
National Orange Showgrounds
San Bernadino, CA
(323) 560-7469

Santa Monica Outdoor Antique and Collectible Market
Santa Monica Airport
Santa Monica, CA
(213) 933-2511

Treasure Island Flea Market
Treasure Island
San Francisco, CA
(415) 255-1923

Ventura Flea Market & Swap Meet
Seaside Park
10 West Harbor
Ventura, CA
(323) 560-7469

The Flea Market
5225 East Platte Avenue
Colorado Springs, CO
(719) 380-8599

Farmington Antiques Weekend
Farmington Polo Grounds
Farmington, CT
www.farmington-antiques.com
(860) 677-7862

Lakewood Antiques Market
Lakewood Fairgrounds
Atlanta, GA
(404) 622-4488

Scott Antique Market
Atlanta Exposition Center
Atlanta, GA
(404) 366-0833

Aloha Flea Market
Aloha Stadium
Honolulu, HI
(808) 486-1529

Shipshewana Antique Auction and Flea Market
Highway 5
Shipshewana, IN
(219) 768-4129

Brimfield Antiques Show
Route 20
Brimfield, MA
(413) 283-6149

Lambertville Antique Market
Route 29
Lambertville, NJ
(609) 397-0456

Englishtown Auction Sales
Englishtown, NJ
www.englishtownauction.com
(732) 446-9644

Great American Antiquefest
Liverpool, NY
(315) 652-1723

Annex Antiques Fair and Flea Market
6th Avenue & 26th Street
New York, NY
(212) 243-5343

Metrolina Expo
7100 North Statesville Road
Charlotte, NC
(800) 824-3770

Picc-a-dilly Flea Market
Lane County Fairgrounds
Eugene, OR
(541) 683-5589

Tennessee State Fairgrounds Flea Market
Tennessee State Fairgrounds
Nashville, TN
(615) 862-5016

replacement services

Alexis Antiques
6348 S. Rosebury
Clayton, MO 63105
www.alexisantiques.com
(877) WEDGWOOD
Wedgwood matching

Fiesta Dish
(860) 675-3159
Fiestaware

Fulbreit China Locators
1688 Autumn Avenue
Memphis, TN 38112
(901) 274-6868
Fiesta, Homer Laughlin, and Metlox, among others

Network Pattern Matching
209 North Ashley Street
Valdosta, GA 31061
www.networkpatternmatching.com
(888) 242-0094

Replacements, Ltd.
P.O. Box 26029
Greensboro, NC 27420
www.setyourtable.com
(800) 737-5223
Matching and repairing of discontinued and hard-to-find patterns

restoration/repair

CP Restoration
6 South 3rd Avenue
Taftville, CT 06380
(860) 886-1870
(800) 882-1870

Harry Eberhardt & Son, Inc.
2010 Walnut Street
Philadelphia, PA 19103
(215) 568-4144
Dealer and restorer of porcelain, glassware, etc.

Farah's Antiques and Porcelain Restoration
1001 West Loop North
Houston, TX 77055
(713) 684-4609

credits

So many wonderful, creative people have brought us into their homes to inspire you and me. I would like to thank them all from the bottom of my heart. Mary

PHOTOGRAPHY ON PAGES 13, 25, AND 67 BY CHERYL DALTON; PAGE 66 BY BRAD SIMMONS. ALL OTHER PHOTOGRAPHY BY BARBARA ELLIOTT MARTIN.

2   HOMEOWNER: Barbara Ashford, Birmingham, Alabama

6   HOMEOWNER: Mary Engelbreit, St. Louis, Missouri

9   HOMEOWNER: Ruth Touhill, Dutzow, Missouri

10   HOMEOWNER: Mary Engelbreit, St. Louis, Missouri

12   HOMEOWNERS: Nancy and Bill James, St. Louis, Missouri

13   top—HOMEOWNERS: Jane and Steve Keltner, Memphis, Tennessee bottom—HOMEOWNER: Susan Welsh, Atlanta, Georgia

14   1960s commemorative plates from Stone Ledge Antiques and Tommy T's; see Getting the Goods

15   HOMEOWNERS: Becky and Louis Portera, Seaside, Florida

16   HOMEOWNER: Rose Hicks, Fredericksburg, Texas

18   HOMEOWNER: Rose Hicks, Fredericksburg, Texas

19   creamware plate at center from Guilford Forge Heirlooms, (203) 453-1618 or (800) 717-4135

20   HOMEOWNER: Rose Hicks, Fredericksburg, Texas

22   HOMEOWNER: Jaime Pliego, Pasadena, California

24   HOMEOWNER: Sheila Griesedieck, St. Louis, Missouri

25   HOMEOWNER: Krista Suechting, Atlanta, Georgia; DESIGNER: Wendy Middleton

26   HOMEOWNER: Joan Zischke, Carmel, California

29   HOMEOWNER: Marcy Spanogle, St. Louis, Missouri; china from Emma Bridgewater, www.bridgewater-pottery.com

30   HOMEOWNERS: Becky and Louis Portera, Dallas, Texas

31   HOMEOWNER: Suzy Grote, St. Louis, Missouri

32   HOMEOWNER: Belinda Hare, Fredericksburg, Texas

33   HOMEOWNER: Mary Engelbreit, St. Louis, Missouri

34   HOMEOWNER: Marcy Spanogle, St. Louis, Missouri; plates from Jill Rosenwald for Tabula Tua, (773) 525-3500